Dropshipping

Step-by-Step Guide to $10,000 per Month in 10 Weeks or Less

By Mark Bresett

Copyright 2016 by Mark Bresett - All rights reserved.

The following book is reproduced below with the goal of providing information that is as accurate and reliable as possible. Regardless, purchasing this book can be seen as consent to the fact that both the publisher and the author of this book are in no way experts on the topics discussed within and that any recommendations or suggestions that are made herein are for entertainment purposes only. Professionals should be consulted as needed prior to undertaking any of the action endorsed herein.

This declaration is deemed fair and valid by both the American Bar Association and the Committee of Publishers Association and is legally binding throughout the United States.

Furthermore, the transmission, duplication or reproduction of any of the following work including specific information will be considered an illegal act irrespective of if it is done electronically or in print. This extends to creating a secondary or tertiary copy of the work or a recorded copy and is only allowed with express written consent from the Publisher. All additional right reserved.

The information in the following pages is broadly considered to be a truthful and accurate account of facts and as such any inattention, use or misuse of the information in question by the reader will render any resulting actions solely under their purview. There are no scenarios in which the publisher or the original author of this work can be in any fashion deemed liable for any hardship or damages that may befall them after undertaking information described herein.

Additionally, the information in the following pages is intended only for informational purposes and should thus be thought of as universal. As befitting its nature, it is presented without assurance regarding its prolonged validity or interim quality. Trademarks that are mentioned are done without written consent and can in no way be considered an endorsement from the trademark holder.

Table of Contents

Introduction 1

Chapter 1: Dropshipping Basics 5

Chapter 2: Discovering Your Niche 11

Chapter 3: Figuring Out How to Use Shopify 19

Chapter 4: Integrating Shopify with Oberlo 27

Chapter 5: Information Regarding Fulfillment by Amazon 35

Chapter 6: Facebook Ad Campaign Cost and Basic Information . 41

Chapter 7: Developing Facebook Ad Sets and Technical Advertising Topics 47

Conclusion 55

Introduction

Congratulations on purchasing your personal copy of *Dropshipping: Step-by-Step Guide to $10,000 per Month in 10 Weeks or Less*. Thank you for doing so.

The following chapters are going to provide you with crucial information regarding how to set up a dropshipping business for yourself that will lead to tremendous profit. If you're currently weary about whether or not dropshipping can be profitable for your wallet and bottom line, considering the following factors will help you to see why dropshipping works in today's technological world:

1. The Internet Has Connected Us All

Like never before in the history of the world, the internet has enabled people to connect with one another in the fastest way possible. This not only has to do with the rise of the internet alone, but also the rise of mobile users on Smartphones and tablets. In fact, from 2007 to 2015, statistics suggest that mobile use of the internet grew from 200 million users to a whopping 1,600 million users. That's truly a remarkable increase. As our internet devices become smaller, it appears that use of the internet grows larger than what anyone could have anticipated. For this reason, considering opening a dropshipping business for yourself should be exciting. You have the potential to reach literally millions of people through their thumbs when they're on their mobile devices.

2. Data Has Never Been So Accessible

Another reason why opening a dropshipping business is enticing to many people is because of the fact that in today's world you're actually able to target the types of people who are more likely to use your dropshipping service. Both Facebook advertising and other types of advertising such as Google AdWords have made this type of marketing possible. When you use Facebook and Google AdWords marketing tools, you're able to see how many people are reacting to the ads that you're posting. With these data analytic tools that these advertising services are able to provide, you get to see how well your ads are doing so that you can tweak them whenever necessary.

3. Inventory is Never a Problem

For traditional businesses, the need to have certain items in stock at all times can pose a problem for two distinct reasons. Firstly, holding inventory requires a certain amount of space. If you don't own a warehouse or have enough storage space in your current home to account for this inventory, then you're going to run into problems. Another reason why holding inventory can prove to be troublesome is because when you purchase physical inventory for your business, you're essentially turning your money into a tangible product. What if your inventory never sells? Then you're going to be stuck with too many products of a similar type and won't be able to do anything with them. For this reason, most businesses would rather hold liquid wealth, rather than wealth in the form of a good that they've purchased ahead of time.

Dropshipping solves both of these problems. As you're going to find as you read this book, dropshipping does not require that you have a warehouse full of goods to ship to your customers, or even that you make the products that you ship yourself. Instead, dropshipping enables you to simply purchase goods from other vendors that you will then ship to your customers, or use warehouses that already exist for your storing needs. In this way, you're able to reap the benefits that exist when you ship products to your customers, without having to worry about the inventory problems that were just discussed in the previous paragraph. With services like AliExpress (which we'll talk about more in this book), you're able to avoid problems associated with inventory. What this essentially means is more liquidity for your business.

4. You Don't Have to be a Tech Guru

Some internet endeavors require that you know some coding language, or at least have some technical knowledge under your belt. With dropshipping, it's nothing like that. Today, services such as Shopify and Amazon FBA allow you to develop a dropshipping business in the easiest way possible. We're going to get into how to do this on both of these platforms, but it's important to understand that with Amazon FBA, setting up a dropshipping business is as simple as setting up an online portal for yourself from which your business can operate. With dropshipping being easier to do than ever before, this is yet another reason why it can be beneficial to your pursuit of greater income. Additionally, this means that you mostly have to worry about finding the best product to sell that will lead to the ultimate profit.

Now that you understand the basic pillars of why dropshipping can be a great business opportunity for yourself right now, it's time to learn a whole lot more! There are plenty of books on this subject on the market, thanks again for choosing this one! Every effort was made to ensure it is full of as much useful information as possible, please enjoy!

Chapter 1
Dropshipping Basics

Before we get into developing your understanding of how to grow your profits on the web, it's important that you understand what dropshipping is. This chapter is going to talk about what the dropshipping supply chain is, so that you fully understand where you fall in this supply chain as someone who is interested in dropshipping yourself. As you're going to see after reading this chapter, there is great profit to be had within the dropshipping supply chain, as long as you know where to position yourself and your business. Let's take a look at these dropshipping supply chain components now.

Dropshipping Entity 1: The Creator of the Product

Also known as the manufacturer, the first entity involved in a dropshipping supply chain is the person or company that creates the product in the hopes of generating a profit from its sale. Even though the manufacturer is likely to offer great deals on their products, they will usually only do this in bulk. Typically, a manufacturer is going to sell to what's known as a vendor or wholesaler, because they know that these types of companies will be able to sell large amounts of their product quickly. Unless you already have a ton of money and know that the product is going to sell well on the internet, purchasing from the manufacturer is not going to be preferable to an aspiring small-business owner such as yourself. This is because it's unlikely that you will have the space to hold this much inventory during a single period of time.

Dropshipping Entity 2: The Vendor

After the manufacturer, the next dropshipping supply chain entity is known as the vendor. The vendor is the point in the supply chain that will sell the products that the manufacturer has made to large retail stores in order to make a profit. In order to make a profit, the vendor will need to raise the price of the product when they sell it to a retail store. Still, it's not recommended that you look at your dropshipping business as being able to compete at the vendor level, at least not on its onset. The amount of product that these vendors are able to sell is quite large, and many times these vendors will even have contracts with the companies to whom they're selling. Unless you already have contacts that will be able to procure you these types of deals, being a vendor is also not in your best interest.

Dropshipping Entity 3: The Seller

Since you're most likely not going to be the manufacturer or the vendor, the place that your business will likely fit best is within the seller portion of the supply chain. The seller can be best described as an individual or small business who purchases the product from the vendor. The seller makes his or her profit by making sure that the price at which they're selling the product to their customers is higher than the price at which they bought it. This is an important concept to understand in regard to developing an online dropshipping business, because if you end up selling your products at a price that is similar to or lower than the price at which you bought the product yourself, making a profit will be nearly impossible. A common percentage that can be used when you're considering how much you want to increase the price of a product by is either 1.5 or 1.6 percent. Of course, you can adjust this percentage as you see fit for your individual business.

Negotiating with Manufacturers, Vendors, and Other Sellers

As you should be able to see from the description of each aspect of the supply chain above, you, the dropshipping entity, is mostly going to exist within the selling portion of the supply chain model; however, this does not mean that the potential does not exist for you to interact with all three of these dropshipping entities along the supply chain in some manner. A key aspect of any dropshipping business is figuring out which manufacturers and vendors will agree to ship their products to your customers *on your behalf.* In other words, instead of having a manufacturer or a vendor ship their products to you so that you can then ship to your customer, some manufacturers and vendors will agree to ship to other people for you, free of charge.

Dropshipping is Not Just a Product-Focused Business

Because of the fact that the customer is going to go through your dropshipping business, it essentially means that he or she does not have to interact with a large and sometimes-overwhelmingly slow manufacturer. This positions the dropshipper as a business that is simply serving as a point of contact for a customer, so that he or she does not have to go through the manufacturer or the vendor themselves. With this being the case, it's important to understand that any dropshipping business is a service, rather than an operation that simply buys and then re-sells products. Without having good customer service, even a reputable dropshipping service is likely to go out of business. It's extremely important to keep this in mind, because excellent client communication is a key element to any good dropshipping business.

Beware of Fees

In addition to communication being a pillar of a reliable dropshipping business, it's also important to point out from the onset that any manufacturer or vendor that tries to charge you a fee in order to dropship with them should not be trusted. There are plenty of legitimate companies that will dropship product for you without requiring that you pay them a fee in return. While this may change as the prevalence of dropshipping becomes greater, for now this is simply not the case. If you do find a company or two that is trying to charge you a fee in order to dropship, you should look elsewhere. If the product niche that you choose is incredibly small, then you might be stuck dealing with these companies that charge a fee, but for a majority of product markets you should be able to find other companies that will provide you with their services for free. Don't be afraid to shop around prior to choosing from whom you're going to purchase your product.

You Don't Need to Develop Your Own Product

The last important point that this chapter will make is that when you create a dropshipping company for yourself, you're able to bypass the actual creation of your own product. Instead, you're able to reap some profit from companies that are already making these products. This is a big reason why dropshipping has become so popular recently. If you don't actually have to think of a product to create, then why would you? Learning how to dropship is thus an exciting alternative to what can otherwise be an incredibly stressful and time-consuming process. Of course, that's not to say that developing a dropshipping business isn't a sometimes-stressful endeavor, but it is arguably a less arduous endeavor than is developing a completely new product for sale from scratch.

This chapter has looked at the basics of dropshipping, and has included details into what dropshipping is and how a dropshipping supply chain works. Understanding the basic components of traditional dropshipping will allow you to feel more comfortable with the market that you're planning to enter. Even though the possibility of online dropshipping has made it easier than ever before to develop a business, the basics of dropshipping are still largely physical, rather than digital, nature.

In other words, if you don't use Shopify or Amazon FBA in order to dropship, it's going to require that you pick up your telephone and physically speak with someone from the manufacturer or vending company. I know, talking on the phone seems so outdated, but with dropshipping you may have to negotiate in this manner. Even if you use Amazon FBA or Shopify, you may still find that talking on the phone with the manufacturer will allow you to develop relationships with the company that you would otherwise be unable to cultivate. In understanding traditional dropshipping, it will be easier for you to integrate old methods of dropshipping with newer digital methods.

Chapter 2
Discovering Your Niche

Now that you know the basic pillars of dropshipping, it's time to turn our attention to more detailed and nuanced aspects of it. The first step to developing your dropshipping company, prior to even developing a website for yourself or a dropshipping portal on Amazon or Shopify, is to figure out the niche market that you're going to be targeting. That's what this chapter will cover. After reading this chapter, you will understand both simple and more complicated tactics that you can use to go about finding the right product to sell online. When it comes to the internet, it's definately true that not all products are created equally.

Why is Finding a Niche Product Important?

Before we get into specific techniques that you can use to find a niche product to dropship to your customers, you need to understand why finding your niche is necessary. In fact, I'll go so far as to say that finding a niche product to sell is not simply necessary, but essential to the prowess of your dropshipping business. Let's take a look at some of the reasons why developing a niche is so important:

Reason 1 to Find Your Niche: The Big Corporations Already Have the Majority of the Business

The first reason why you need to find a niche for your business is because most large corporations have already cornered large swaths of a market with their products. For example, if you were to decide that you were going to start dropshipping all athletic clothing, then you would be competing with giant sport company conglomerates including Nike, Under Armour, and Adidas. For many small dropshipping businesses, they find more success in targeting the products that they offer around smaller niches. This way, they are able to corner this particular market. This would mean that instead of targeting all sports clothing, it might be more advantageous for a dropshipping company to only target running shoes for example, or another type of niche like basketballs of all shapes and sizes.

Reason 2 to Find Your Niche: You Can Center Your Niche Around Keyword Research

Many online business, dropshipping in nature or not, choose to develop their business around keyword research that they've done. This is also known as SEO, or Search Engine Optimization. Every time that anyone in the world types a search into a search engine, like Google or Bing, this information is documented and recorded. If you were looking to develop a niche dropshipping business, you could subscribe to an SEO tool on the internet that could then tell you which keywords are being searched most often. If you were to do this, you would want to look for keywords that have a high search level, but are not being targeted by many other online businesses. Most SEO tools will be able to provide you with information regarding how competitive the keyword in which you're interested is.

Reason 3 to Find Your Niche: It's Easier to Market to People

When you're able to find a niche that's profitable, it's also going to be easier to market to your intended audience. Anyone who has taken a basic marketing class knows that understanding your audience is one of the key ways to properly market to people in a way that will lead to conversions. Once you know the types of people who are interested in purchasing the products that you're selling and dropshipping, you will be able to create ads that will lead to greater sales. Online marketing can often be an essential part to growing your business, as long as you know what you're doing. We will be dedicating an entire chapter of this book to understanding how you can develop a successful Facebook ad campaign for yourself. For now, it's simply important to understand that marketing can either make or break your online business.

Now that you're aware of three primary reasons why a niche product is important to have when you're starting your dropshipping business, we will now get into some ways that you can find a niche product for yourself. We have already loosely discussed one, it being that you can use SEO marketing tools on the web to enhance your keyword research. Some other tactics that you can use when you're looking to find a niche market include the following:

1. Check Out Magazines:

While magazines largely make their money through the subscriptions that their readers pay, another essential way that these magazines make their money is through the products that they promote. For example, if you've ever flipped through a magazine and have thought that there are far too many advertisements in it, then it's safe to say that the magazine that you're looking through gets a lot of money from the advertisements that they feature. While this fact may mean that you have too many pages to flip through in order to get to some readable content, it also means that from a research perspective, this magazine may benefit you more than you think. Remember, these advertisers would not be buying ad spots in magazines if they did not think that the ads would lead to sales.

Another important tip that goes along with looking through the advertisements that you see in ads is to be on the lookout for ads that are enticing to you personally. While yes, a business should be as emotionless as possible, your dropshipping business should also sell products about which you're somewhat passionate. For example, if you decide that you're going to sell tires online because your research suggests that they will sell well but you hate cars in general, then this may not be the best option for you. If you can find a happy medium between a product that will profitable and a product that you will also enjoy selling, that would be ideal. Of course, if your goal is to make as much money as you can, then this advice may be lost on you; however, it can be argued that enjoying what you're doing should be a part of any business endeavor that you take on.

2. Find a Niche through Amazon:

Whenever you search on Amazon to buy something, they are going to provide you with results that are based on "relevance". What many people do not know is that you can change this search requirement to a few other options. These options will allow you to see which products are the most popular within a niche that you're researching. For example, in addition to the "relevance" search, some other search requirements that you can set instead include the following:

- Price: Low to High

- Price: High to Low

- Avg. Customer Review

- Newest Arrivals

Personally, when I'm searching for products that I want to purchase for myself, I will always change the search to the "Price: Low to High" setting, but this is not the best option for someone who is trying to find a dropshipping niche. Instead, it would be the most beneficial for you to set your Amazon search to "Avg. Customer Review". After you've set your search parameters to this, the next step is to look for all of the products that have a 5-star review next to them. You also want to make sure that the product in question has a lot of reviews. If you choose a product to sell that only has one 5-star review, this does not guarantee that many people find it particularly useful or popular.

In addition to looking for products with at least one hundred reviews with a 4.5 star rating or better, you can also type in "Best Sellers on Amazon" in the Amazon search bar. Doing this is going to allow you to see the top 100 most popular Amazon products on a given day. If you have no idea what your niche is going to be, then doing this will be able to provide you with an adequate understanding of what's selling the most on Amazon. With Amazon being one of the most commonly used consumer platforms on the market today, it's obvious that this information could be extremely useful as you try to figure out what your niche market is going to be.

3. Complement Your Amazon Research with Research on AliExpress

After you've done research in both magazines and on Amazon, you shouldn't consider your work to be finished. One last way that you can find your dropshipping niche involves doing research on the AliExpress shopping platform as well. Similar to Amazon, this site allows you to simply type in "Best Selling Products". Once you type this into the search engine, you will be shown the best products that are currently selling on AliExpress. After you've done this, perhaps you will be able to cross reference the best-selling products on AliExpress with the best selling products on Amazon. You may be surprised to find that some of the best-selling products on Amazon are also being sold on AliExpress. If this is the case, then it should be an indicator that you should make this particular product part of your niche market.

This chapter should have been able to convince you of the importance of developing a dropshipping business around some sort of niche market. Without a niche, your business is likely going to drown amidst competition that is far too strong in relation to the small operation that you plan on running. Of course, it's also important to point out that there are plenty of people on the internet who say that a niche market is going to limit your business potential. It's important to consider both sides of this argument while you're developing your business; however, this book ultimately suggests that a niche product market is the way to go.

Chapter 3
Figuring Out How to Use Shopify

As should be obvious after reading the previous chapter, finding a niche for your dropshipping business is of the utmost importance if you want to be successful. After you've patiently taken the time to find a niche of products that you're relatively sure will sell well, your next step is to start developing your selling platform. One way that you can do this is through a website that's known as Shopify. This chapter will go through how you can setup a Shopify account for yourself in a step-by-step fashion, and will also discuss some of the finer points of Shopify such as cost of use.

The Cost of Shopify

Before we get into how to set up your Shopify account, we should first go over how much this service cost. Remember, applications like Shopify and Amazon FBA are going to allow you to bypass having to learn any programming or website configuration techniques; however, this convenience is not going to come without a cost. As it currently stands, Shopify prices its services at the following cost, depending on the type of account that you choose to open. Additionally, the cost of Shopify is going to depend on whether you plan on allowing credit card transactions, and whether or not you're going to be using Shopify in a physical store or strictly online. It's more than likely that you're going to be using Shopify strictly over the internet, but if you decide that you're going to be using Shopify in a brick-and-mortar store, know that this is going to influence how much you have to pay for it. This book is going to discuss how much online payments cost on Shopify, because this is most likely how you're going to be using the Shopify portal. A breakdown of the cost of using Shopify can be seen below:

The Most Basic Account: The most basic Shopify account is going to cost you $29 per month. If you're business is only going to be online, then any credit card transactions that you complete for your customers on Shopify is going to cost you 2.9% of their total cost, along with an additional 30 cents. In addition to charging a credit card transaction fee, receiving money from your customers in the form of PayPal or another type of transaction tool is going to cost you another 2.0%.

The Middle-of the-Road Account: If you're willing to pay $79 per month instead of $29 per month, you're going to benefit from only being charged 2.6% on any transaction that is made with a credit card plus an additional 30 cents. Using external payment methods like PayPal will only cost you 1% instead of 2%.

The Most Expensive Account: The most expensive account that Shopify offers is going to cost you a whopping $300 per month. Credit card transactions will cost an additional 2.4% with the same 30-cent charge that has been seen in the two other account types. Lastly, you will only have to pay .5% on any money that is gained through mechanisms like PayPal.

As you can see from the description of each account-type price above, the phrase, "You have to spend money in order to make money" is true even when it comes to developing an online dropshipping business. If you ultimately become sure that you want to open a Shopify account for your business, you need to think about how much you're going to charge your customers based on the amount of money that you're going to be paying Shopify each and every month. For example, you can certainly add the percentage cost of a transaction fee into the price of the product that you're selling, but if the price of the product becomes too high then it's likely that your customer is going to look elsewhere for it. Now that you understand the pricing that's involved with opening a Shopify account, we will now go through all of the steps that you need to take in order to open one up for yourself.

Step 1 to Using Shopify: Figure Out How You're Going to Be Using the Shopify Application

This first step involves figuring out how you're going to be using Shopify, based on the information that was presented in terms of price along with a few other factors. When you're first starting to use Shopify, it's recommended that you start with the $29 option. This way, if it turns out that you don't like the

Shopify platform, you won't be spending almost $100 to figure it out. In addition to figuring out the type of account you're going to open, Shopify is also going to ask you questions relating to taxes. Your answer to these questions will depend on the state in which you'll be doing business.

Shopify will also want to know how much money you plan on earning with your account with them. You should try to answer this question to the best of your ability. To answer this in the most accurate way possible, you will first need to figure out the price that you're going to charge for each of your products. You should take your account type into consideration when you're determining this number. After you've calculated what you're going to charge for a particular product, your next step should be to divide this number into the average amount of profit that you think you're going to see from the difference between how much you're going to be paying for the product and how much profit you're going to be making by selling it.

For example, let's say that Emily decides that she's going to sell top-of-the-line party hats (they're gold-plated and Kim Kardashian has made them wildly popular) on her dropshipping Shopify site. She has negotiated a deal with the manufacturer of these party hats and will have to pay $80 per hat. After she adds in the credit card operating costs and her monthly $29 subscription to the Shopify site, she decides that she's going to sell each of these hats on her site for an even $130. To figure out the percentage of profit that she's going to see from selling these hats, she will have to do the following equation:

$80/$130 = .615%

By dividing her cost for the hat by the price at which she's going to sell the hat, Emily is on the road to making nearly a 62% profit per hat that she sells. In dollars, this comes to $50 profit per hat. In my opinion, that's not too shabby. The next step would be to simply try and anticipate how many hats she plans to sell throughout the year. This will largely depend on how popular the product is that she's selling, and how well she's able to market her product.

One final thing that should be mentioned in regard to understanding your dropshipping businesses' profitability is that it's never a bad idea to consider establishing some sort of business plan for your business, even its loosely defined. This way, you will be able to formally document things such as your businesses' potential earnings based on empirical research that you've done beforehand.

Step 2 to Using Shopify: Sign Up

After you've taken some time to think about how you're going to be using your Shopify profile the next step is to sign up for your Shopify account. You do this similarly to how you would open up an account on any other type of application. Go to Shopify's website and move towards the Start link on their page.

Shopify is then going to ask you for the email address that you'd like to have associated with your dropshipping business. For this reason, you may want to think about setting up a professional email account for your website prior to signing up for Shopify. Gmail allows you to make an email account for free. This way, you can be more organized, and this will also allow you to have an email address that resembles the name of your business.

Step 3 to Using Shopify: Put the Items that You're Selling Up for Sale

Shopify will provide you with a page where you can upload pictures of all of the items that you're selling. Once uploaded, you will also be able to add photo descriptions and prices for all of the items that you're selling. In this day in age, the importance of uploading a photograph for each and every product that you're planning to sell cannot be overstated. It's been proven that people are much less likely to purchase your products if there is not a photo to go along with it. Since you're going into the business of dropshipping, this means that you may not have the products that you're selling in your own personal possession. To avoid breaking any copyright infringement laws, it's recommended that you either make sure that the photos that you're uploading are free for anyone to use, or you contact the manufacturer and see if they have any stock photos that they can send you.

Step 4 to Using Shopify: Develop Your Platform's Theme

Next, you're going to want to customize your Shopify platform. You want to make your site as appealing as it possibly can be. To do this, all you have to do is go to the page within Shopify that's titled, "Customize Your Site". You can change how your site looks based on simple prompts within this page, and can even see your changes for review before you apply them in real-time.

Step 5 to Using Shopify: Decide How You're Going to Make It Rain

You also have to consider how your business is going to process credit card payments. If you remember from earlier in this chapter, Shopify is going to charge you if you decide that you want to use a payment processor that isn't theirs. Yes, Shopify can offer you their own payment processor, but if you're more comfortable using a different one than you may end up ultimately paying the fee that they charge to use an external processor.

Step 6 to Using Shopify: Figure Out Your Domain

In addition to being able to provide you with a payment processor, Shopify also offers its users the choice to purchase a domain name from them if they choose to do so for $9.00. A domain name is going to be the website name that your Shopify account gets. If you choose to buy a domain name through Shopify, what it essentially means is that Shopify technically owns your site. To remind you of this, your Shopify domain name is going to resemble the following:

FancyPartyHats.shopify.com

As you can see from the example above, the ".shopify" portion of that URL is not something that every single website has. If you want to avoid that type of wording on your page's URL, then you should look into purchasing a domain name from another site, like GoDaddy.com. From there, you can transfer the domain name that you purchased to your Shopify account.

Chapter 4
Integrating Shopify with Oberlo

Now that you have an understanding of how you can go about setting up a Shopify account, we are going to get into how you can design your Shopify account in a way that will truly enhance it for dropshipping purposes. After reading this chapter, you will fully understand what Oberlo is if you've never heard of it before, and how you can use Oberlo in a way that will maximize your goals and make your dropshipping business maximally profitable.

A Little About Oberlo

Oberlo is a platform that is all for trying to help dropshipping companies with their business. The primary way that they do this is by avoiding the traditional inventory practices that online businesses will typically use. These traditional practices of housing inventory in large warehouses and distributing them accordingly was already discussed at length in chapter 1. Instead of requiring a small business to purchase inventory or negotiate with dropshipping companies to find one that will work for them, Oberlo bypasses all of that. With Oberlo, you're able to easily add products to your product inventory in your Shopify portal, without having to worry about the dropshipping details behind the product you're advertising. Instead, Oberlo handles the backend of every order that is placed on your Shopify site. In fact, Oberlo is able to *automatically* fulfill an order that someone has placed on your website. Let's take a look at some of the other features that Oberlo can offer a dropshipping business:

1. **Automatic Restock:** When you integrate Oberlo into your Shopify profile, it's going to automatically update the inventory status on your Shopify account for you. For example, if someone else on Oberlo or AliExpress sells out of their product, an "out of stock" label is going to appear on the product on your website.

2. **Orders are Fulfilled for You:** When a customer purchases a product from your site, you're going to be notified, but you don't have to worry about dropping whatever you're doing and attending to the order that was just fulfilled immediately. When you use Oberlo, the order process is taken care of for you. Once your customer finishes the purchasing process, Oberlo will package, ship and email the customer, letting them know that their order was successfully placed. This allows for greater comfort for both you and them.

3. **It's Free to Use:** Another great perk about Oberlo is that it's free to install! Unlike Shopify, Oberlo does not charge you any fees while you're using it, which makes importing goods onto your site truly a breeze.

How to Install Oberlo

Now that you've read about some of the advantages of using Oberlo, you might be thinking to yourself, "where do I sign up!" Well, that's also incredibly simple. All you have to do is go to

Integrating Shopify with Oberlo

Oberlo.com. On its homepage, you're going to see a blue button that says, "Add Oberlo to Shopify". Click on this button, even if you do not yet have a Shopify account. From here, Oberlo provides you with two options. These options are, "Create a Shopify store" and "Connect your Shopify store". Choose the option that is best suited for your situation. It's that simple!

The Google Chrome Oberlo Extension

Once your Shopify website is connected to your Oberlo account, Oberlo will then ask you if you'd like to install Oberlo's Chrome Extension. This extension is what is going to allow you to import goods directly from AliExpress into your online store, and then fulfill your customer's orders more easily. The Chrome Extension option is going to be located at the top of your Oberlo screen on the right-hand side, after Oberlo has been added to your Shopify account. Go through the installation process first. Next, you may want to change the settings on your Chrome Extension. To do this, simply look to the right-hand side of the website search engine bar on the Chrome interface. If you've done everything correctly, you're going to see Oberlo's logo, a blue and white sale icon there. Click on this icon, and a dropdown menu will appear. This dropdown menu will allow you to choose certain settings for when you're importing products into Shopify. Some of these options include the following:

1. **Your preferred shipping method:** If you're selling your products to mostly US residents, then Epacket is most likely going to be the easiest and cheapest shipping option for you.

2. **The Country You're from Which You're Doing Business:** This option provides information regarding where you're shipping from so that shipping rates can be correctly provided to your customer.

3. **The Type of Currency You'd like to Display:** The currency option is going to allow you to choose the type of currency you'd like the price of your products to be displayed in.

How to Import Products Directly from Oberlo's Website

Once you install Oberlo, you will be able to import products to your Shopify profile in one of two ways. These two ways include choosing from products on Oberlo's website, and choosing products from AliExpress' website. We will go through how to import products from both sources. To import products from Oberlo's site, start by typing the type of product for which you're looking into Oberlo's search bar. From here, you will be taken to a list of products that matches your search's query. Next, click on an item that interests you and that you'd like to feature on your site. Next to the product's photo on the right-hand side, you will see a green button that says, "Add to Import List". Click on this button, and then you can continue looking for other products that you'd like to add to your online store.

Once you've found a couple of products and have added them to your import list, the next step is to import them into your site. To do this, hover your mouse over the second menu icon on the left-hand side of the Oberlo menu. This icon is underneath of the icon of the graph. Choose the option that says, "Import List". This will take you to a page where all of the items that you've added to your import list can be seen. From here, you can change the descriptions of your products so that they're uniquely yours. You can also choose the collection that you'd like to see them in on your Shopify site, as well as add some keyword tags that might be helpful in generating interested individuals to your site.

How to Import Products from AliExpress

Another option that you have when it comes to importing goods to your Shopify profile is to do so through AliExpress. Make sure that you've downloaded the Chrome extension for Oberlo prior to doing this, and that you're also importing goods from a Google Chrome web browser as well. The first step to importing goods from AliExpress is to head to the AliExpress website. Next, type the product type that you'd like to search for in AliExpress's search engine. Find a product that you'd like to import, and click on this product. From here, you're going to see a blue tag appear in the right-hand corner of the product's image. Click on this blue tag. Do this as many times as you'd like on the AliExpress site. When you're ready, head back to Oberlo. Go to your import list, and you will see all of the items that you've chosen from AliExpress in this portal. Next, perform the same actions that you did when adding products to Shopify via Oberlo. Change the description of the product to your liking, and add product tags as necessary.

Some Final Thoughts on AliExpress

As you can see, shipping products from AliExpress via Oberlo is incredibly simple. Oberlo essentially allows you to only spend your time worry about which products you're going to add to your page. There are few things that you need to keep in mind during this process:

1. **Don't Ship Products from China:** If you find that a certain vendor on AliExpress is faster than others, then perhaps you can break this rule, but for the most part you should try to stick to this principle whenever you can. While your customer may be willing to wait for their product for two weeks or longer, sometimes dropshipping products to your customer from China can lead to unpredictable shipping times. For this reason, it's generally recommended that you stay away from featuring products that are being shipped from China on your page.

2. **Get Some Tracking Software:** In addition to the Chrome extension, another good tool to have at your disposal would be a shipment tracking application of some kind. This way, both you can your customers will have completely transparent information when it comes to when their product is going to

be delivered to them. Some good tracking applications that work well with Shopify include Shippo, Trackr, and DevCloud.

3. **Oberlo Isn't *Always* Free:** Oberlo is free to use for the first 500 products that you sell, and as long as you're selling less than fifty products per month, it's going to remain free to use. Once you've sold 500 products or are selling more than fifty products per month, it's going to cost you around $30 for a basic Oberlo account. When you're first starting out, 500 products can seem like a number that you're never going to reach. By the time you've hit 500 product sales, you'll likely be better at operating Shopify and Oberlo, and the $30 per month will not seem like a very steep price to pay.

Chapter 5
Information Regarding Fulfillment by Amazon

As you can see from the two previous chapters, Shopify can provide you with many great tools that you can use in order to take your dropshipping business to the next level; however, in addition to Shopify, there are other tools out there that will allow you to develop a dropshipping business without necessarily knowing any computer code or language. Another type of tool that can help you achieve your dropshipping business goals is known as Fulfillment by Amazon, or Amazon FBA. This chapter is going to discuss how you can get the most from an Amazon FBA account, so that you can then decide if you'd prefer to use Shopify or Amazon FBA, or even a combination of the two.

The Cost of Using Amazon FBA

Before we get into how Amazon FBA works and how you can sign up, it's important that you understand the cost of participating in the Amazon FBA program. As it currently stands, Amazon FBA requires you to pay a monthly fee of $40 per month. This can be a steep price to pay, especially for someone who is just starting out getting his or her dropshipping business together. In addition to this $40 monthly fee, you're also going to be charged a transaction fee every time you make a sale through Amazon's website. Specifically, Amazon is going to charge you 99 cents every time you make a sale on their site.

The Primary Amazon FBA Advantage

The primary advantage of doing business through Amazon FBA is the hope that you'll be able to save money on shipping costs. As you're going to see, you need to physically ship your products to Amazon in order to work with Amazon FBA. In other words, Amazon is agreeing to be your warehouse for you. This is much different from a Shopify account, where you don't need to physically have your products at any time. Because you have to ship your products to Amazon, the idea is that you can save money on shipping materials and the cost of shipping the item itself because Amazon is always going to use the "Best Method" of shipping your product to your customer.

Obviously, these prices are a bit steeper than the ones that we saw for a Shopify subscription. Why then, would anyone opt to use Amazon FBA for their dropshipping business? Let's take a look at some of the perks that Amazon FBA can offer its users that Shopify simply cannot.

1. **Amazon's Client Base is Larger:** Firstly, Amazon knows that it's arguably the largest and most popular product web browsers in the entire world. They know that if individuals are able to sell on their platform, sales are likely. This reasoning can allude to one reason why the price of Amazon FBA might be a bit more expensive than other online dropshipping platforms out there.

2. **You Don't Necessarily Need a Site:** Another reason why people flock to Amazon FBA for their dropshipping business is because you don't need an online store at all in order to start using Amazon FBA. As you're going to see once we start discussing how to use Amazon FBA, by focusing your energy on your brand's image, you will be able to create an identity for your business with absolutely needing to create a website; however, a website might be helpful for your overall sales.

3. **The Products You Send Amazon are Truly Yours:** When you send products to an Amazon warehouse, you can still gain access to them at any time. This means that if you are an Amazon FBA subscriber, but also have your own online store on other sites like Shopify or Etsy, Amazon will gladly ship your products back to you if and when you make a sale on these other sites. For this reason, Amazon FBA can be a great way to give your products greater exposure if you have more than one online store up and running. In this way, Amazon FBA is able to be used as an integration tool with any other business platforms that you're running.

How to Use Amazon FBA

Now that you're aware of some of the benefits that Amazon FBA can provide to a dropshipping entrepreneur like yourself, we will now get into how you can go about getting an Amazon FBA account up and running. To do this, you should follow these steps:

1. **Sign Up for an Amazon FBA Account:** To do this, go to www.services.amazon.com. You can also type in "sign up for Amazon FBA" into Google to access signing up that way. From here, follow the prompted steps that you'll need to perform in order to get yourself an Amazon Seller Central Account. Once the registration process has been completed, you can then start adding products to your Amazon FBA selling-central page.

2. **Sign Up for Amazon's Marketplace Web Services:** Amazon's Marketplace Web Services can be best defined as an integration tool that can enhance the profitability of your account with Amazon FBA. Specifically, you're able to manage your inventory, download order information, and receive report information whenever you want to with this free tool.

   To sign up for Amazon Marketplace Web Services, go to User Permissions within the Amazon FBA selling portal. From here, click on "Get Credentials". Next, click on "I want to get my credentials for accessing my own Amazon seller account with Amazon." That's all there is to it. You can think of Amazon Marketplace Web Services as being similar to the graphs of data that Shopify provides you with. Not everyone knows that Amazon provides this portal to its sellers. Unlike Shopify's data tools, Amazon's are less well known.

3. **Add Your Distributor:** Because you're going to be sending products to Amazon, but you want to do it via dropshipping, you will need to add a distributor to your Amazon FBA

portal. This way, Amazon will know with somewhat security that you're going to be able to fulfill your products to your customers. To do this, perform the following steps:

- Go to Settings, then General then Distributors

- Press "+add" and then add the name of your distributor

- Press "+add" and the company's name

    Obviously, this is going to require some legwork on your end. You will need to negotiate with a dropshipping service that will agree to ship your products to Amazon for you. Contrastingly, you can also opt to try and deal with the direct manufacturer of the products that you're looking to sell, to see if they will ship items to Amazon on your behalf for free. If you can achieve this, you will save yourself a lot of money in shipping costs.

4. **Set Your Distributor Record as "Dropshipper":** This step is pretty self-explanatory. You want Amazon to know that you're going to be dropshipping your products to them.

5. **Configure the FBA Plugin:** The FBA plugin is going to configure your computer to be optimized for Amazon FBA selling. On the left side of the FBA selling center, click on Modules. From here, find the module that's called "Fulfillment by Amazon". Next, click settings, and then "enable". Next, specify your settings for Amazon FBA, including your shipping preferences. The shipping preference options include

Standard shipping, Expedited shipping, and Priority shipping. Obviously, the cost of each of these shipping methods is going to go up depending on what you choose.

6. **Start Putting Products in Your Portal:** Finally, you will be ready to start uploading photos of your products to your FBA selling portal.

This chapter should have been able to provide you with basic information on how to use Amazon FBA. If you're not completely sold on the advantages the Amazon FBA can offer your dropshipping business, then you can certainly bypass using it completely and still develop a successful dropshipping business through Shopify and Oberlo. Additionally, it's important to keep in mind that you should find products that are going to profitable, prior to signing up for Amazon FBA.

Chapter 6
Facebook Ad Campaign Cost and Basic Information

By now it should be obvious that you're going to find the most success with your dropshipping business when you're able to advertise the products that you're selling effectively. The best way to do this is to try and reach millions of people who are eager and ready to purchase products with the click of a button. One platform that has these types of people ready and waiting to purchase products that are advertised to them is Facebook. This chapter is going to discuss how you can advertise to people who subscribe to Facebook in the most effective way possible. If you can figure out how to target specific people who are most likely going to be interested in what you're selling, you'll be able to increase your conversion rates and make more money.

How Much Does Advertising with Facebook Cost?

When you think of doing business with Facebook, you may think that this means that you will be spending an arm and a leg because Facebook is such a large enterprise. The reality is that you'd be surprised how far your money can go with a Facebook ad campaign. On average, it's going to cost you around 65 cents per click for United States advertising. To look at it in a different way, if you spend sixty-five dollars on a Facebook ad campaign, you're going to pay 65 cents per 100 clicks.

The 65-cent count is an average estimate of how much someone is going to pay when they're advertising on Facebook. The reality is that depending on the industry that the products that you're selling falls under, it's going to depend on how much you pay per click. Below is a breakdown of an average cost of how much a Facebook ad is going to cost per click (CPC), depending on the industry in which you're advertising:

Industry	Advertisement Cost-Per-Click
Technology	$1.28
Real Estate	$1.80
Health Products	$1.30
Household Goods	$2.90
Workout and Wellness	$1.90
Education	$1.01
Beauty Products	$1.80
Auto Repair Gear	$2.25
Clothing	$.50

This information regarding how much an ad is going to cost on a per-industry basis should at least be somewhat considered while you're choosing which products you're going to sell on your dropshipping site. These advertising costs are going to influence how much money you make through your dropshipping site, and for this reason you should be trying to keep these costs as low as possible. That being said, it does not mean that you should seek to spend no money on advertising. That would be a grave error; however, the initial product research that you do and the industry that you eventually choose for your products should be somewhat dictated by your advertising costs.

How to Create a Facebook Ad Campaign

To get started using Facebook advertising, the first thing that you're going to want to do is head to www.facebook.com/advertising. From here, click on "create an ad". Please note that you will also have to own a Facebook account prior to implementing this step. If you don't already have a Facebook account, you need to sign up for one. Once you finish the process of signing up for Facebook ads, you will then be asked whether you're interested in creating advertisements or what are known as sponsored stories.

A Quick Detour…Understanding Sponsored Stories

Sponsored stories can be defined as ads that disguise themselves in the form of Facebook news feed information. For example, if you're browsing your Facebook feed and receive a notification that your friend Michelle recently "liked" a local business called Ed's Tire Repair Service, it's important to understand that you did not receive this information by accident. This means that Ed's Tire Repair Service has chosen to advertise its page as a sponsored story on Facebook, in the hope of generating "likes" and growing its clientele. Sponsored stories are most frequently used to promote others to like a page, but some other ways that they can be used include advertising when your Facebook friend's check-in to certain places or when an individual post that a company published is liked as well.

Back to the Main Program…

After you choose whether you're going to use traditional advertising techniques or sponsored stories, the next step is to choose where people are going to go once they click on your advertisement. In order to provide Facebook with this information, you will have to give them a URL. For the purposes of your dropshipping business, it would be best to send your potential customers to your Shopify online store. Additionally, regardless of whether you decide to promote your business using traditional advertisements or sponsored stories, it would probably benefit your business if you created a Facebook page for it. This way, people can "like" what you're promoting, even if you're not advertising these likes each time someone does.

Creating Your Facebook Ad

Once you've gone through the process of setting up a Facebook ad campaign account, you then have to start thinking about how you're going to go about configuring your ad. Below are some guidelines that will help you through this process:

1. **Decide on Your Landing Page:** This is the page that potential customers will see once they click on your ad. Are you going to send them to your site's home page so that they can browse all of your products? Or are you going to send them to the page where a specific product can be purchased so that they spend less time browsing and more time clicking 'add to cart"?

2. **Decide on the Title:** Also known as the headline, the title should include words that are going to entice your consumer to click on your ad in the first place. Your title should be short and to the point, and should cater to the *true motives* of your consumer. What's in it for them if they click on your ad and purchase product from you?

3. **Decide on an Image:** Every advertisement that you make as part of your Facebook ad campaign should have an image to go with it, no exceptions. Choose an image that is equally as enticing as your ad's title.

4. **Decide on the Body Copy:** After deciding on the title and the image that you're going to use for your ad, the next

important feature to include is the ad's body copy. This writing should provide a description of what you're advertising, and why your customer should care.

Once you've developed your ad and it looks aesthetically pleasing, you can upload it to your Facebook ad campaign portal. At this point, Facebook will also provide you with the option of previewing your ad to make sure that you like how it looks within the Facebook application. If there is something in the preview that you didn't consider beforehand, you can then edit your ad prior to it going live.

Chapter 7
Developing Facebook Ad Sets and Technical Advertising Topics

Now that you understand the basic tenets of how to sign up to start configuring Facebook ad campaigns for your business, and also have an awareness of what makes an effective advertisement, this chapter is going to focus on the more technical aspects surrounding how to develop not just any Facebook advertisements, but effective ones that are sure to grow your business. This chapter is going to get into how to develop a Facebook ad campaign, how one ad can work for multiple types of people to whom you're marketing, and will also provide you with information regarding ad sets.

Various Ways to Target Your Market

If you're familiar at all with Google AdWords, then the concepts surrounding Facebook ad targeting will probably seem familiar because both Google AdWords and Facebook advertising work quite similarly. Once you develop the ad that you're going to be using on Facebook, you can then target the types of people that you want to reach in a variety of ways. Some of these ways include the following:

- Demographics
- Location

- People's Interests

- People's Behaviors

Since you're someone who is primarily concerned with dropshipping, location targeting will probably not be beneficial for you, since you are looking to target anyone on the internet rather than in one specific area of the world; however, an aspect of Facebook targeting still revolves around where in the world you'd like your ads to be seen. For most people who are reading this book, you will likely set this option to the United States.

The options that you have when it comes to demographics includes your audience's age range, as well as their sex. This can definitely come in handy when you're looking to target specific types of people for a particular product. For example, if you're interested in selling beard grooming products to men, then you would probably want to set your age range for this particular ad to be between the ages of 16 years old and "any". The any option means that anyone over the age of 16 years old is eligible to see your ad while you're on Facebook. There is also an option within this section of Facebook advertising that includes advanced options such as sexual orientation, marital status, language, level of education, and career choice.

Setting Your Facebook Advertising Budget

Once you've set up how you'd like to target your audience for a given ad that you've uploaded to Facebook, the next step is to set up your budget. To do this for a particular ad campaign that you're starting, head to "Pricing" and then "Set a Different Bid" in the Advanced section of the pricing window. From here, you will be able to set a bid price for your advertisement based on ads that are similar to yours given all of the options that you've chosen for it.

It's important to understand the notion of bidding when it comes to Facebook advertising before moving forward. Depending on the specific criteria that you've set for your ad, the competition for getting the best placement within Facebook is going to vary in price. For example, let's go back to beards. Facebook's data analysis knows which male Facebook users between the ages of 16 to 100 years old are the most likely to purchase grooming kits from the advertisements that are placed on their Facebook dashboards, based on these user's past activity. Thus, when you place a bid for your ad, you're essentially competing for a spot within the best advertising spots that Facebook has. It's also important to understand that simply setting your ad's price at an enormously high rate is going to guarantee that your ad is going to be picked first. The quality of the ad, the effectiveness of the ad's title, and the image associated with the ad, are all also going to be taken into consideration during the selection process.

After you decide at what price you're going to place your bid, the next decision to make has to do with the pricing structure for your ad. The two most popular options for Facebook ads include cost-per-click (CPC) and cost-per-impressions (CPM). For most Facebook advertisers, CPC is going to be a better option because CPM will only guarantee that 100 people *see* your ad on their feed, while CPC means that you are only going to pay when someone *clicks* your ad. After you've chosen the type of ad campaign you're going to run, you can review your ad and tweak it as needed. That's the gist of what Facebook can offer you in terms of effective advertising.

Advanced Facebook Ad Configuration: Ad Groups

After reading through all of the steps that you need to take in order to effectively upload a single advertisement to Facebook, you would be right to think that this can be a rather tedious process. Instead of doing this for every single ad that you create, Facebook also offers you the option to instead compile ads of a similar nature into what's known as an ad group. An ad group can be best defined as a group of advertisements that all have the same parameters set for a group of advertisements that you choose to group together.

The Facebook Power Editor

When you're looking to create not just ad groups but also entire ad campaigns that will ultimately help you to execute your Facebook marketing pursuits more effectively, then the Facebook

Developing Facebook Ad Sets and Technical Advertising Topics

Power Editor is a tool that is essential. This tool will allow you to edit, create and publish several ads at the same time, while also having control over the campaign itself. Let's take a look at how you can develop ad campaigns and ad groups with the Power Editor by your side. To download the Power Editor, make sure that you're on a Google Chrome web browser. Next, simply type in "Power Editor" in the Facebook search engine and download the plugin from there.

The Hierarchy of an Ad Campaign

Once you've downloaded the Power Editor, you will be ready to create campaigns. You should think about an ad campaign as being structured in a hierarchical fashion. At the top, you have the campaign. Beneath that, you have your ad sets (also known as groups), and within these groups are the individual ads that you're planning to use with similar criteria associated to each ad within a specific group. It's safe to say that you're never going to feel limited in your ability to create ad sets within a Facebook campaign, since you are able to create up to 1,000 campaigns and ad sets, with up to 5,000 ads per your entire Facebook advertising account.

Campaign Criteria:

At the top of the hierarchy, you're going to first set up the objectives or advertising goals that you have. These objectives are going to apply to all of your ads, regardless of the set that you end up putting them in. Some of the objective choices that you have include the following:

1. Video placement

2. Engagement with apps

3. Page likes

4. Conversions

5. Clicks to your online store

To set up a campaign, simply go to the "Campaigns" tab within the Power Editor. Next, provide your campaign with a name. That's all there is to it.

Ad Sets within Your Campaign

The next step it to set up your ad sets. To do this, select the campaign that your ad sets are going to fall under. Click "View Ad Sets" and then the "+" option so that you can add a set. Next, give your ad set a name. Once you've set up an add set, you're going to need to consider your objectives that you have for that particular set. These considerations include the following:

1. **Your Ad Schedule:** When is this ad set going to start, and when is it going to end? What times during the day do you want the ads within this set to run?

2. **Your Ad Budget:** Determine your daily budget.

3. **Your Bidding Options:** This choice will either be between CPC or CPM.

4. **Ad Targeting:** Each ad set is going to target one group of people that you determine for it.

5. **Ad Placement:** Do you want your ads to appear on mobile phones and tablets, or on desktop computers? Do you want them to appear on someone's Facebook newsfeed, or on the right and left-hand sides of the screen?

Once you've determined the types of parameters you'd like each of your ad sets to have, the last step that you have to take involves adding advertisements to your ad sets. To do this, go to "View Ads" within your campaign and specific ad set. From here, click the "+" button, just like you did when you were looking to add a campaign and an ad set to your Power Editor profile.

A Final Thought on Facebook Advertising

There were a lot of important advertising steps that were presented in this book that you need to consider. With a dropshipping business, advertising is going to make or break your business, because advertising effectively is likely going to be the only way that you can generate more business for yourself. It's extremely important to remain diligent and persistent when you first get started advertising on Facebook. You're going to have to be prepared for a lot of experimentation so that you can find what works and what doesn't for the particular groups of people that you're targeting. The formula that you should keep in mind is finding the sweet spot that works for your specific audience based on the product that you're selling and the type of ad that you're producing. Keep this in mind as you move through the experimentation process, and don't give up, even when you want to!

Conclusion

Thank for making it through to the end of *Step-by-Step Guide to $10,000 per Month in 10 Weeks or Less*. Hopefully, you feel as if this book has provided you with the tools that you need to succeed in order to start a profitable dropshipping business. Remember, the internet has made it more possible than ever before to an eager and infinite audience. With the tools that were discussed in this book at your disposal, developing an internet empire for yourself has never been easier.

The next step is to starting using the tactics that this book acquainted you with! Figure out whether you want to start using Amazon FBA or Shopify, and go from there. Contrastingly, if you decide that you ultimately want to develop your own niche website for your dropshipping business, the information in this book will still be useful! Be sure to develop your business in a way that best suits your individual strengths as both a business owner and internet consumer. If you develop your business around what you're good at, success is much more likely. Lastly, good luck!

Finally, if you found this book useful in anyway, a review on Amazon is always appreciated! Thanks again for downloading this book *Step-by-Step Guide to $10,000 per Month in 10 Weeks or Less*!

www.ingramcontent.com/pod-product-compliance
Lightning Source LLC
Chambersburg PA
CBHW050022230526
45470CB00003B/1084